CW01207413

OXFORD
UNIVERSITY PRESS

Great Clarendon Street, Oxford, OX2 6DP, United Kingdom

Oxford University Press is a department of the University of Oxford. It furthers the University's objective of excellence in research, scholarship, and education by publishing worldwide. Oxford is a registered trade mark of Oxford University Press in the UK and in certain other countries

Text © Oxford University Press 2023

The moral rights of the author have been asserted

First Edition published in 2023

All rights reserved. No part of this publication may be reproduced, stored in a retrieval system, or transmitted, in any form or by any means, without the prior permission in writing of Oxford University Press, or as expressly permitted by law, by licence or under terms agreed with the appropriate reprographics rights organization. Enquiries concerning reproduction outside the scope of the above should be sent to the Rights Department, Oxford University Press, at the address above.

You must not circulate this work in any other form and you must impose this same condition on any acquirer

British Library Cataloguing in Publication Data

Data available

ISBN: 978-1-382-04348-9

10 9 8 7 6 5 4 3 2

The manufacturing process conforms to the environmental regulations of the country of origin.

Printed in China by Golden Cup

Acknowledgements

The Toxic Spider and *Electric Animals* written by Benjamin Hulme-Cross

Content on pages 10, 41 and 42 written by Suzy Ditchburn

Illustrated by Vincent Batignole, Kate McLelland and Q2A Media Services Pvt Ltd

Author photo courtesy of Benjamin-Hulme Cross

The publisher and authors would like to thank the following for permission to use photographs and other copyright material:

Back cover: Ken Kiefer 2 / Image Source / Getty Images. Photos: p6: OUP, p7, 45(tl), 46: wildestanimal / Shutterstock; p44(t): Mochipet / Shutterstock; p44(ml): Vector things / Shutterstock; p44(mr): vasabii / Shutterstock; p44(b): James Osmond / Photodisc / Getty; p45(tr), 52: Lukas Vejrik / Shutterstock; p45(ml), 57: Antagain / E+ / Getty Images; p45(mr), 54, 55: imageBROKER / Alamy Stock Photo; p45(bl), 63: Milan Zygmunt / Shutterstock; p45(br), 65: Alexander Oganezov / Shutterstock; p47: BigBlueFun / 500px / Getty; p49: Ken Kiefer 2 / Image Source / Getty Images; p50: Sail Far Dive Deep / Shutterstock; p51: Rob Atherton / Shutterstock; p53: Martin Pelanek / Shutterstock; p54: OUP, p56: AzmanL / E+ / Getty Images; p58: Billy Hustace / The Image Bank Unreleased/Getty Images; p60(t): DKeith / Shutterstock; p60(b): Lea Rae / Shutterstock; p61: Geza Farkas / Shutterstock; p64: Dave Denby Photography / Shutterstock; p66: Sue Robinson / Shutterstock; p66-67: arqramos / Shutterstock.

Every effort has been made to contact copyright holders of material reproduced in this book. Any omissions will be rectified in subsequent printings if notice is given to the publisher.

MIX
Paper | Supporting responsible forestry
FSC™ C110497
www.fsc.org

In this book ...

The Toxic Spider 11

Electric Animals 43

Have a go!

or as in world

ear as in search

ou as in soup

oul as in shoulder

ie as in field

ve as in groove

y as in bicycle

are as in share

ere as in there

ear as in bear

tch as in patch

because

6

Read this book if ...

you like

SLIMY SPIDERS

or

SHOCKING SHARKS!

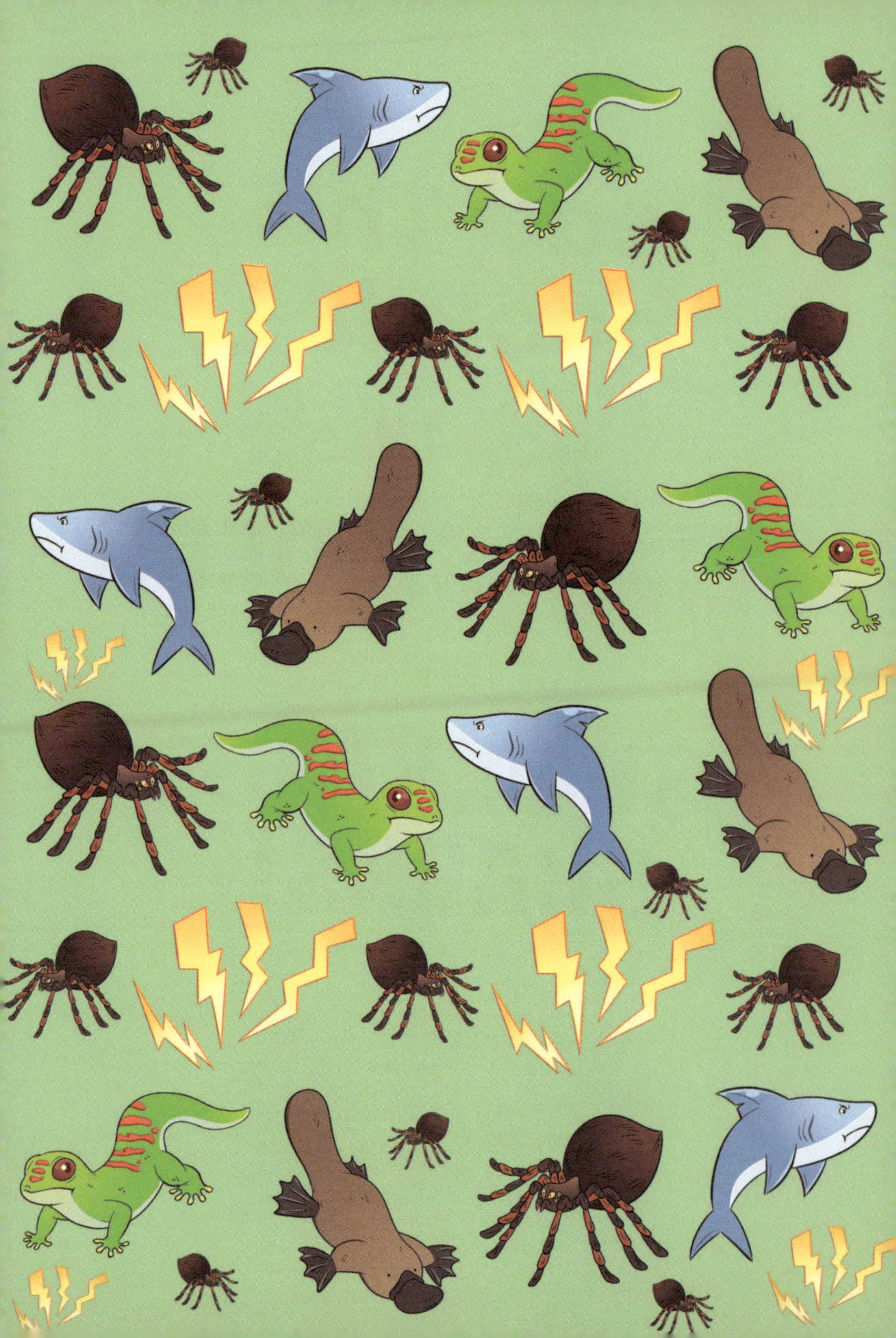

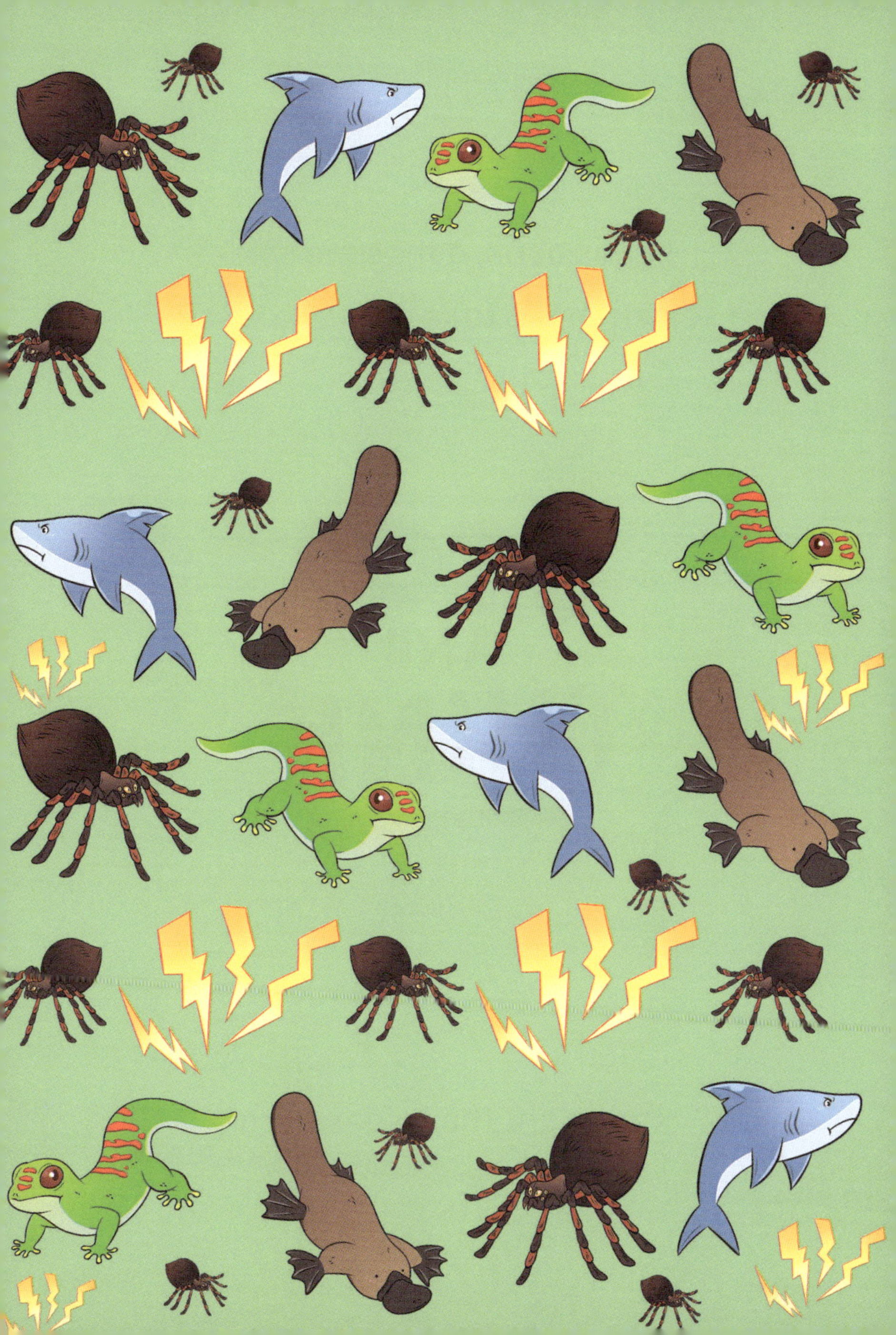

In this book, a massive spider attempts to take over at a disco.

STOP AND THINK

How might the spider do this?

ISAAC AND THE TOXICS

THE TOXIC SPIDER

Written by Benjamin Hulme-Cross
Illustrated by Vincent Batignole

Isaac
(say: igh-zuk)

Anna

Mr Woolly

Filip

Head of the Toxics: she wants to take over the town.

Toxic spider

Isaac loves experiments. He must use them to defeat the Toxics. His mates Anna and Filip help.

"Don't be afraid, I will not **zap** you!" Isaac said.

He was ready to show everyone his experiment in the school hall.

"Isaac is going to test which things conduct electricity," said Mr Woolly. "Are you ready, Isaac?"

"**Ready!**" said Isaac.

"Electricity can only pass along some objects," said Isaac. "They are called **conductors**. You need a battery, lightbulb and wires with clips. You also need some objects to test."

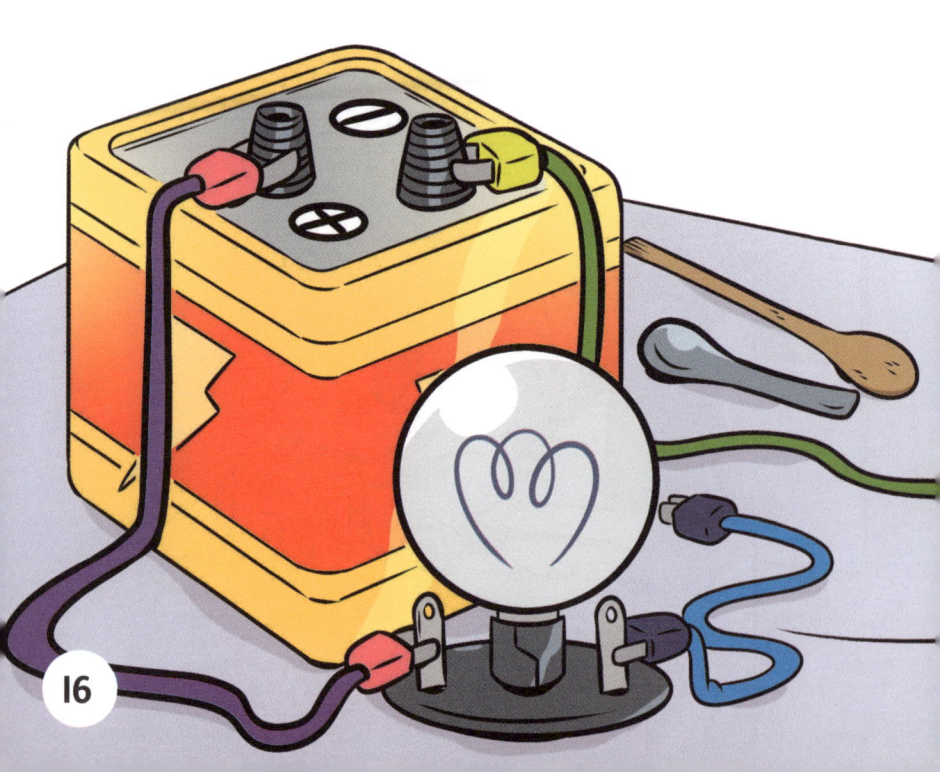

"Connecting the clips to a metal spoon makes the bulb glow," said Isaac. "It will not work with a wooden spoon."

"Is it because metal is a **conductor** and wood is not?" Filip asked.

"Correct!" said Isaac.

"Good experiment, Isaac," said Mr Woolly. "That's all for today."

"Yes!" Anna said. "It's time for the end-of-term disco!"

LATER ...

"This is going to be so cool!" said Filip.

They were on their way to the disco. They didn't see the

MASSIVE SPIDER!

Inside, the music was very **LOUD**.

Filip offered his sweets.

Isaac got a prize in a **name the bear contest!**

The three of them jumped and twirled without a care in the world.

Lights lit up the room in blue and purple. Behind them, the spider **glowed green**.

Suddenly, one of the lights **POPPED** and went out. Soon, most of the lights were out.

"Look over there!" Anna shouted.

24

"A SPIDER!" yelled Isaac.

"It's **massive!**" said Filip. "It's shooting **green slime** at the wires!"

"That can only mean one thing," said Anna.

"It's a **TOXIC ROBOT!**" they all said together.

"We have to stop it!" said Isaac.

"Where did it go?" said Filip.

They spotted the massive spider. It was running around in the shadows.

"It's made of metal nails!" said Anna with a **shudder**.

Isaac watched as the **Toxic spider** flung a massive slime ball at a light.

The last of the lights went **POP!** Someone **screamed**.

"What are we going to do?" cried Filip.

"In my video game you **ZAP** the robots," said Anna.

"The robot spider is **metal!**" said Filip. "We learned that metal conducts electricity!"

"That's it!" Isaac shouted.

32

"We need to connect the spider to my battery!" said Isaac. "It might have the power to **zap** the robot's microchip. It would shut it down."

Suddenly, Mr Woolly appeared.

"What on earth is that thing?" he cried.

"It's a Toxic spider. We need to **zap** it," said Isaac.

"Leave the zapping to me!" said Mr Woolly.

35

"Get the spider to come here!" Mr Woolly shouted over his shoulder.

He spread out Isaac's battery and wires. He started connecting them up.

Isaac approached the spider.

"Over here!" he shouted.

The spider ran over. Its metal legs **tap-tap-tapped**.

Isaac ran up to Mr Woolly. The spider was right behind him.

"**NOW!**" Isaac yelled.

Mr Woolly clipped Isaac's wires onto the spider.

The spider stopped. Its **green glow** got stronger. It was burning up inside! At last, the spider crumbled into a pile of scrap metal.

"Your experiment worked!" said Mr Woolly. "**Fantastic!**"

"What a relief! We defeated the **nasty Toxics** again!" said Isaac, grinning.

Look back

1. What did Isaac win at the disco?

2. Is wood or metal the best conductor of electricity?

3. How do you think the friends feel after defeating the Toxic spider?

In this book, we look at how animals use electricity.

STOP AND THINK

Why do you think animals use electricity?

ELECTRIC ANIMALS

Written by Benjamin Hulme-Cross
Illustrated by Vincent Batignole

Contents

Electricity in the wild 44
Hunting 46
Shocking 54
Solar powered 60
Gripping 63
Catching 65
You are electric! 68
Glossary and Index 69

Electricity in the wild

We use electricity to **power** computers. We use it to **light up** our homes. We even use it to **power** cars.

Are you aware that some animals use electricity too?

- shark
- platypus
- Atlantic torpedo ray
- electric eel
- gecko
- spider

Hunting

Some animals use electricity to *hunt* their **prey**. Sharks can detect electricity in the *water*.

How can this help a shark hunt? Fish make tiny amounts of electricity when they swim.

Sharks detect this electricity and find the fish.

SHOCKING FACT

Sharks can detect electricity in the water from over 900 miles away! That's as far as from Scotland to Spain!

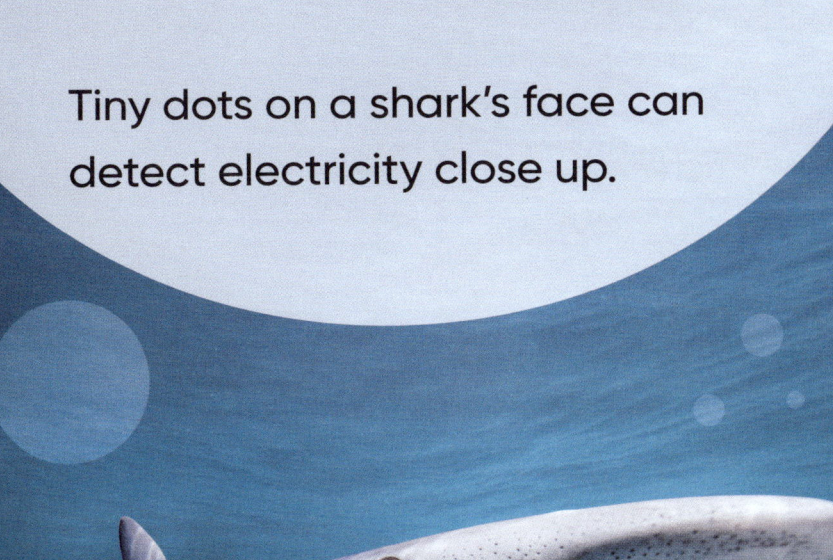

Tiny dots on a shark's face can detect electricity close up.

Look at all the dots on this blue shark's face!

These dots can help sharks find fish hiding under the sand!

Sharks are fantastic at **smelling** fish, too. So, there is no place to hide for the sharks' prey!

The platypus likes to eat worms and shellfish. These produce electricity. The platypus scans the riverbed with its bill. It detects the electricity to find its dinner!

bill

SHOCKING FACT

A platypus has 40 000 **sensors** in its bill. This helps it to find its prey!

Shocking

Some animals give out a **massive** electric shock to stun their prey. The Atlantic torpedo ray makes its own electricity. It keeps the electricity like a battery.

The ray hides and waits for prey to come near. Then the ray suddenly stuns it with a **BIG** electric shock.

Fishing boats catch torpedo rays in nets accidentally. When they free the rays, the workers are careful. They wear protective gear, but can still get a nasty shock!

The biggest shocker of all is the **electric eel**.

SHOCKING FACT

The electric eel isn't an eel at all!

The electric eel can give a **massive** electric shock. It's over **three times stronger** than the electricity in our homes.

SHOCKING FACT

Electric eels can be very **long!**

I'm taller than you!

Solar powered

This bug can even use its body like a **solar panel**.

solar panel

60

This hornet traps light from the sun. It turns it into electricity in its body.

Experts think these hornets use the electricity for power.

SHOCKING FACT

In the past, experts believed that only plants could make electricity from light. This hornet has made experts learn something new!

Gripping

Some animals use electricity to **grip** onto things. Electricity helps this gecko to cling on as it travels.

A gecko has electricity in its toe pads. This helps it stick to smooth walls.

toe pad

Catching

Spiders' webs use electricity. The webs are coated in a *sticky glue*. This glue **conducts** electricity.

SHOCKING FACT

The electricity in a web helps to grab insects flying near it!

The webs also grab dirt. Experts can check the webs to see how clean the air is.

You are electric!

Your nerves send electric signals to your brain. That is how you understand what is going on. Electricity makes everything you think, dream and do possible.

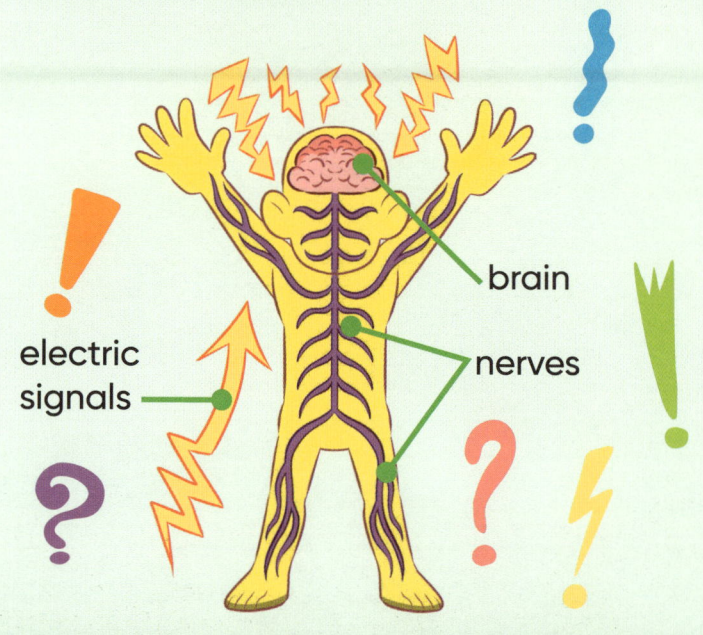

electric signals

brain

nerves

Glossary

conducts: allows electricity to pass along it

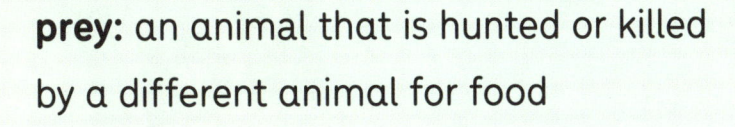

prey: an animal that is hunted or killed by a different animal for food

sensors: organs that detect things like light, heat or electricity

solar panel: this converts the sun's power into electricity

Index

electric eel 57–59
gecko 63–64
hornet 60–62
platypus 52–53
shark 46–51

Ha! Ha!

What did the fish say when it saw an electric eel?

I'm shocked!